Reducing Anger

Harnessing Passion and Fury to Work for You – Not Against Others

Dale R. Olen, Ph.D.

A Life Skills Series Book

JODA Communications, Ltd.
Milwaukee, Wisconsin

Editor: Carolyn Kott Washburne
Design: Chris Roerden and Associates
Layout: Eileen Olen

ISBN 1-56583-009-1

Published by: JODA Communications, Ltd.
                10125 West North Avenue
                Milwaukee, WI 53226

PRINTED IN THE UNITED STATES OF AMERICA

Table of Contents

Introduction

to the
Life Skills Series

N obody gets out alive! It isn't easy navigating your way through life. Your relationships, parents, marriage children, job, school, church–all make big demands on you. Sometimes you feel rather ill-equipped to make this journey. You feel as if you have been tossed out in the cold without even a warm jacket. Life's journey demands considerable skill. Navigating the sometimes smooth, other times treacherous journey calls for a wide variety of tools and talents. When the ride feels like a sailboat pushed by a gentle breeze, slicing through the still waters, you go with the flow. You live naturally with the skills already developed.

But other times (and these other times can make you forget the smooth sailing), the sea turns. The boat shifts violently, driven by the waves' force. At those stormy moments, you look at your personal resources, and they just don't seem sufficient.

Gabriel Marcel, the French philosopher, wrote that the journey of life is like a spiral. The Greeks, he observed, viewed life as *cyclical*–sort of the same old thing over and over. The seasons came, went, and came again. History repeated itself. The Hebrews, on the other hand, saw life as *linear*–a pretty straight march toward a goal. You begin at the Alpha point and end at Omega. It's as simple as that.

Marcel combined the two views by capturing the goal-oriented optimism of the Hebrews and the sobering reality of the Greeks' cycles. Life has its ups and downs, but it always moves forward.

To minimize the *downs* and to make the most of the *ups*, you need **Life Skills**. When you hike down the Grand Canyon, you use particular muscles in your back and legs. And when you trudge up the Canyon, you use other muscles. So too with life skills. You call on certain skills when your life spirals down, such as the skill of defeating depression and managing stress. When your life is on an upswing, you will employ skills like thinking reasonably and meeting life head on.

This series is about the skills you need for getting through life. To get from beginning to end without falling flat on your face and to achieve some dignity and some self-satisfaction, you need basic life skills. These include:

1. Accepting yourself.
2. Thinking reasonably.
3. Meeting life head on.

With these three life skills mastered to some degree, you can get a handle on your life. Now, if you want to build from there, you are going to need a few special skills. These include:

4. Communicating.
5. Managing stress.
6. Being intimate.
7. Resolving conflict.
8. Reducing anger.
9. Overcoming fear.
10. Defeating depression.

If you have these ten skills up and running in your life, you are ready to face yourself, your relationships, your parents, your marriage, your children, your job and even God with the hope of handling whatever comes your way. Without these skills, you are going to bump into one stone wall after another. These skills don't take away the problems, the challenges and the hard times. But they do help you dig out of life's deep trenches and more fully *enjoy* the good times.

Life Skills can be learned. You have what it takes to master each of these skills—even if you feel you don't have the tiniest bit of the skill right now. But nobody can develop the skill for you. You have to take charge and develop it yourself. Your family, friends and community may be able to help you, but you are the center at which each skill has to start. Here is all you need to begin this learning process:

- Awareness.
- The desire to grow.
- Effort and practice.

Awareness begins the process of change. You have to notice yourself, watch your behavior and honestly face your strengths and weaknesses. You have to take stock of each skill and of the obstacles in you that might inhibit its growth.

Once you recognize the value of a skill and focus on it, you have to want to pursue it. The critical principle here, one you will see throughout this series, is *desire*. Your desire will force you to focus on the growing you want to do and keep you going when learning comes hard.

Finally, your *effort and practice* will make these **Life Skills** come alive for you. You can do it. These books are tools to guide and encourage your progress. They are my way of being with you— cheering your efforts. But without your practice, what you find in these books will wash out to sea.

Working on these ten **Life Skills** won't get you through life without any scars. But the effort you put in here will help you measure your life in more than years. Your life will be measured in the zest, faith, love, honesty and generosity you bring to yourself and your relationships.

I can hardly wait for you to get started!

Chapter One

How Anger Works

The work day finally ends. You're driving home through heavy traffic. More trucks out than usual, you think. But who cares. You're on your way to peace and quiet. The day felt long, more meetings than you like. You couldn't get any desk work done. And nothing creative was accomplished. Oh, well, you can tolerate that. As you drive toward your subdivision, a wave of contentment sweeps over you. That's a surprise. You don't get many of those treats. Seems like so much stress lately.

You pull into the driveway but can't park in the garage because the kids' bikes are strewn across the floor. You lay on the horn for a few seconds. No one comes. You beep again. Still no response. You pull on the emergency brake, get out of the car, move the bikes, return to the car and park. That's annoying. They know you come home at this time. The bikes shouldn't be there.

You go into the house. The kids are watching television. You really get irritated now. "Didn't you kids hear me beeping out there?" you demand. "No," they sort of reply. It's more of a grunt than a clear "no." You go into the kitchen, crunching through a little mine field of fallen Rice Krispies. Several used bowls clutter the counter, along with the cereal box and two good-sized milk spills. In the middle of it all sits the cat, enjoying every slurp. She's not even supposed to be on the counter. You hit the ceiling. You yell at the kids to turn off the damn television. They watch way too much of that anyway, you say, especially on such a nice day. They should be outside.

"Get in here and clean this mess up," you shout. You give them the lecture about how you are not their servant and how they have to learn some responsibility. They don't look like they're grieving their serious failure in responsibility. In fact, they look angry with *you*, as though it were your fault. You become even angrier. You begin cursing to make your point more emphatically. Finally, you send them outside where they ought to be anyway, getting fresh air. The house is finally quiet. Then it hits you. You are really angry. Yet you felt so content on the way home.

What got into you? How could you switch from contentment to anger so quickly? How could you lose control? You make that promise to yourself so often, about remaining calm with the kids. Almost every day, though, they catch your anger.

If you have this kind of experience and these kinds of questions, then you've picked up the right book. What causes this anger emotion anyway? Does it have any useful purpose? And most important, how can you reduce your anger when it starts to overtake you?

Certainly you didn't imagine your family life peppered with angry outbursts. In your ideal world you saw yourself coming home from a productive, successful day at the office to a tranquil home, where the aroma of fresh-baked bread filled the house. The kids would be sitting quietly at the kitchen table doing math homework, with the dog sleeping peacefully at their feet. Nothing would be out of place. The snack droppings would have been swept up, the dishwasher cleaned out and the garbage already sitting at the curb. You would have walked in, changed into casual clothes, sat by the window and read the evening newspaper. Ah, what a life it was supposed to be!

Unfortunately, harsh reality smacks you square in the face. In real life it just ain't that way! The kids, the bikes, the dog, your spouse, the house, the weather, the newspaper don't always cooperate. They don't fit your ideal vision of life in your adult world. You respond with anger. When things don't fit your idealized image of the world, anger becomes one of your most common responses. You use it to force that uncooperative world to shape up and fit your view of how life is supposed to flow.

When the world around you doesn't cooperate and fit your master plan, you feel as if you have lost control. You are no longer in charge. You don't like that. You need to regain power. So you use power against power. You get angry in order to take control again.

But a strange thing occurs. Not only do you feel like you've lost control over your world and its behavior, but you also feel like your anger has taken control over you. You even say things like, "I really lost it with the kids tonight." Translated: "My anger had power over me. I felt completely out of control. I couldn't stop myself."

Not only do you want to be in charge of the events around you, but you want to feel in charge of yourself. Perhaps more than any other emotion, you can feel out of control with anger. It seems to have a life of its own. You need to harness it, master it, make it work for you instead of against you. You want to be the master of your anger, not its slave. You can learn to take control of this emotion the more you understand it. The skill of reducing and controlling anger rests on your awareness of it – what it is, how it works, why you feel it and what you can do to control it.

You know what anger is. You feel it coursing through your body. You hear your voice grow louder. You feel your skin tighten and heat up. You sense an inner rush – blood racing through your body. Your mind can't keep up with the wild and bizarre thoughts that trip over each other – violent, revengeful, dramatic. Most of your anger is caused because the real world doesn't fit your picture of the ideal world. And you keep insisting that the real world must change to match the world as you want it.

You have an ideal view of how people should drive their cars. When they don't drive the way you think they ought to, you want to change them. You want to straighten them out on how to drive according to your standards, which are certainly the correct standards. But you can't stop them on the highway, instruct them and expect them to graciously accept your criticism (albeit positive and constructive). You feel helpless. You don't know how to change them. But inside yourself you continue to *demand* that they change. You then become angry with them as your last effort to convert them (even though it has absolutely no effect on them). You also get angry as a way of dismissing their real world so that you can continue to hang onto your ideal world of how driving ought to happen.

Anger contains three elements: adrenaline, a stressful event and triggering thoughts.

Any of these three elements serves as the starting point for anger. The stressful event – the car cutting in front of you – can trigger demanding thoughts about how that person should drive. Those two elements – the stressful event and the triggering thoughts – can spark the flow of adrenaline, giving you the feeling of agitation and anger. Or you could have triggering thoughts about getting to your meeting on time and how important that meeting is. Then the car cuts in front of you (stressful event), leading to the flow of adrenaline. Anger results.

Finally, your adrenaline level might already be high. You just left your office where you had a disagreement with your boss. You feel threatened by what she said. Now you're driving along and the car cuts in front of you. You think, "What a jerk!" and become angry. Inevitably all three of these elements will be present for anger to surface.

Adrenaline

The physical feeling of anger happens because the hormone called *adrenaline* is released throughout the body. This hormone has been viewed, in part, as the "flight-fight" hormone. It gives you added energy and strength when you most need it. Whenever you feel threatened in some way, this hormone is released in your body to help you handle the threat.

When people lived in caves, a lion occasionally approached the community. Adrenaline was immediately released in the cave-dwellers. They had a choice: either they could fight the lion (for which activity they needed additional strength and energy), or they could turn and try to outrun the lion (for which they also needed more strength and energy). Once the threat was over, the adrenal gland slowed down.

That stressful event – where the approaching lion did not *fit well* with the cave people's safety – triggered the flow of adrenaline. Today whenever you experience stress, adrenaline flows throughout your body. It increases diastolic blood pressure, heats up your skin, increases your heart beat and tenses your muscles. With so many stresses touching you every day, you might wonder if adrenaline is flowing all the time. It may well be. Your body can remain in a high state of alert all day, ready to deal with the stresses of modern life. That state of frequent, if not constant, adrenaline flow serves as a basis for your anger.

So you come home from a rather stressful day at work, drive through heavy traffic, see the bikes in the garage, step into the Rice Krispies and blow up at the kids. No wonder. Your "fight-flight" response has been charged all day. The hairtrigger was set from morning on. Now the cannon goes off. Gee, you wonder why? Stressful situations, a lot of adrenaline. Now add some demanding thoughts about how the house and the kids should appear when you arrive home. Mix all those ingredients together, stir constantly and, presto, a zesty dish of anger!

Stressful Events

The second ingredient in a good batch of anger involves those elements that do not fit together when you want them to. These are the stressful events that occur in the real world that don't match your expectations of how life should be. Such events set off your demanding thoughts about how things ought to be. Here are some of the stressors that tend to elicit demanding thoughts and activate the flow of adrenaline:

1. Physical conditions such as cold temperatures, noise, hunger, fatigue and pain.
2. Other people attacking your self-esteem through criticism or rejection.
3. Unjust and unfair treatment by others.
4. Losing your freedom or power to control the things around you.
5. Others not living up to your expectations.

These types of stressful situations play an important part in creating anger. Although by themselves they do not cause anger, when they are mixed with adrenaline and triggering thoughts, anger rises to the surface.

Triggering Thoughts

Until now I've been calling these thoughts "trigger thoughts," because they activate much of the anger you feel. From now on I'd like to call them "anger thoughts," because more often than not that's what they create. You can be sure that if you think in certain demanding and dramatic ways, you will inevitably become angry. Basically, when you create an ideal world and then *insist* that people live according to it, I guarantee that you will become angry.

To understand and manage your anger then, you need to pay attention to the way you think. Your thoughts proceed in the following way:

1. This is the *ideal* world, the world the way I want it to be.
2. But here is the *real* world, and it does not match my *ideal* world.
3. I *demand* and *insist* that the real world measure up to my ideal world.
4. I see that the real world does not budge and move toward my ideal world. It stays where it is, no matter how much I insist it be like my ideal world.
5. I continue demanding that the real meet my ideal, and I think how *terrible* it is that the gap between the two is so *infinitely* wide.
6. I now experience frustration that the real world is not moving according to my demands to be more like my ideal world.
7. There must be something seriously *wrong* with the real world. I *blame* it for not measuring up to my ideal.
8. *Demanding thoughts, dramatic thoughts and blaming thoughts* all descend on the mismatch between the real and ideal worlds. I cannot seem to make the real meet the ideal. I think my ideal world is being *threatened*.
9. With the sense of threat begins the flow of adrenaline. Result: Angry thoughts, the mismatch of the real world with your ideal world and adrenaline all converge and lead to anger.

Three specific thoughts trigger anger – demanding thoughts, dramatic thoughts and blaming thoughts. Let's look at these three thoughts that lead to anger.

Demanding thoughts lead to anger.

Inside of you lives a little "legislator." He goes around the world making up *laws* about how everyone else should behave and how everything else should operate. He can make laws about the weather, the environment, traffic patterns, people's use of time, proper manners, money and even about God. He can also make laws about you: how you should behave, what you should think and how you should feel. This little guy has energy. He rarely takes a recess and stays in session 12 months a year, working right through holidays and late into every night.

Before you go any further, recognize your legislator. See what laws he has made. Take a pencil and paper and jot down all the laws you have made that come to mind. Just listen to your inner speech. Pay attention to the words "should, ought, must and have to." Every time you hear one of those words, write down what comes after it. I'll bet your list goes on and on. Here are some typical laws I hear in myself and in others:

1. People *must* be on time.
2. Kids *shouldn't* be so noisy.
3. The bathroom sink *shouldn't* get plugged up so easily.
4. People *ought* to appreciate how hard I'm working here.
5. My boss *has* to give me a raise.
6. My spouse *ought* to know what my needs are after all these years.
7. No one *should* talk to me with such disrespect.
8. Taxes *should not* keep going up.
9. Dogs *must not* poop in the park, and if they do, owners *ought* to clean up after them.
10. People *should* disregard "call waiting" when I am talking with them on the phone.

These 10 rules and regulations can be multiplied by 100, and you will still not run out of laws. As I said, your little legislator is a busy fellow.

But here's the rub. While you have a lot of *legislative power* and go around making up rules for the world to live by, unfortunately you do not have much *executive power* to enforce the rules. The executive in you would have trouble making the above 10 laws stick. You might be able to get the bathroom sink not to plug up so frequently (number three), but trying to enforce the others laws would be tough, indeed.

Imagine being elected to your state legislature. What an honor. You go to your state capitol and begin hammering out legislation. You make laws. But then you find out there is no *executive* branch of government. Nobody is there to enforce your laws. You would become pretty frustrated as a legislator.

In your personal life you will feel, at times, that your executive branch of government is very weak, even non-existent. The fact is you don't always have the power to control events outside of you. You can make all the laws you want about your friends, family and co-workers, but you can't always make them behave according to your laws. In those cases having legislative power without any executive power dooms you to frustration, which leads you to anger.

Take the first law above: "People must be on time." You can pass that law, but it's pretty tough to enforce it. You can threaten your children about being on time for church or catching the school bus. But they still keep getting in the car at the last minute. And you keep steaming about how irresponsible they are, all the way to church.

Meetings should start on time, right? But what if the boss keeps coming late. You don't have too much executive power to enforce your law. You can see, then, that making laws without having executive power is inherently frustrating. To continue insisting that your laws be obeyed, even when you can't make that happen, is down right maddening.

Demanding that the real world measure up to your ideal world, then, leads you directly into anger. You grew up, for example, learning a model for the ideal marriage. You imagined it to be a total partnership, where the two of you did everything together. You should both get home from work, pitch in to help the kids with homework, get dinner ready, pick up the mail, clean up after the meal, play with the kids, put them to bed, clean the house – all together. Then you should sit down and have an intimate conversation about the day and how much you love each other.

But the reality turns out quite different. Your husband comes home from work, sits down with a drink, reads the paper and waits for you to get dinner ready. Afterwards he retires to the family room for an evening of zoning out in front of the tube. You have to help the kids with homework and make sure they get to bed on time. By nine o'clock you're exhausted, he's sleeping in his chair and the television is droning on.

This isn't exactly how you imagined marriage and family life. As time goes on, you begin to *insist* that he help you and get involved in this family, damn it! He doesn't change. You get more insistent, demanding that he get off his duff. Things improve for a week or so, but soon he's right back in front of the television. You become even more demanding, saying to yourself, to him and to anyone who will listen: "He should, he ought, he must, he has to become a partner with me in this relationship." But he continues doing nothing as you become more insistent that he get involved.

You have much legislative power here but little executive power. You have a stressful situation: your ideal marriage does not match well with your real marriage. You're trying to get your real marriage to move up the ladder to better fit your ideal. You attempt this by *demanding* that the real change to meet the ideal. But, unfortunately, you cannot force the real to change. That stressful situation, plus your ongoing, demanding thoughts, makes you angry.

Dramatic thoughts fuel angry feelings.

You insist that the world should be as you imagine it. You demand, placing your anger under the real world to shove it up toward the ideal.

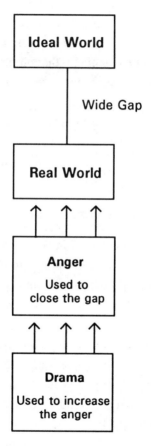

When that doesn't work very well, you add *drama* to your demanding thoughts to pump up your anger. You make your anger bigger, so it has more power. You say things to yourself such as:

"I can't stand this any longer."

"This is the worst thing that could ever happen to me."

"I'm trapped in this relationship forever."

"I'll never recover from this."

"That's the most cruel thing anybody could ever say to
   another human being."

"I absolutely cannot believe she did that."

"I've never seen such stupidity in my entire life."

These are just a few of the hundreds of statements you make to yourself – or to anyone listening – that pump you up. They literally feed the demanding thoughts that create the anger. Reality is so outrageously far from your ideal that you can hardly stand it. Yet dramatic thinking actually creates greater distance between the ideal and real. In turn, such drama aggravates the demanding thoughts and leads to further insistence that the real ought to change. Dramatic thinking fuels the fires of anger.

Blaming thoughts cause anger.

Remember when you were a kid. You'd come home from school with your report card. You'd have pretty good grades, but then there would be that check on the "Deportment" side of the card, next to "Needs improvement in cooperating." When your parents asked you what that was about, you said, "It wasn't me. The kids around me talk all the time, and I get blamed for it." Your parents, wise to the ways of children, responded with something like, "Sure, you did absolutely nothing. You were perfectly innocent." Then you'd get angry with your parents for not believing you and say, "Well, if you don't believe me, then ask my friends if I ever talk in school. I don't. They're the ones who should have gotten the check mark."

My father was a great one for blaming others for his golf game. I loved golfing with him, and I particularly enjoyed how creative he was in blaming others when he made a poor shot. Somebody was moving when he putted. Or someone made a foot print in the path of his ball, or the greens weren't cut short enough. His most creative blaming came one day after he made several poor shots. He was getting quite upset. He explained why he was shooting so poorly. "You know, this is your mother's fault. I was supposed to take her to the beauty shop this morning, and she's wasn't ready in time. Then I had to rush her there and rush here to make our tee time. All that rushing around makes me miss these shots. If she had been on time, I'd be shooting much better."

Blaming helps you explain why the real world does not match up to your ideal world. To get free from the pain and discomfort of a stressful situation, you attempt to make sense out of it. So you ask the question, "Why? Why does the real world here not measure up to my ideal world? And why can't I make my ideal world happen?" One of the easiest answers to the "why" question is blaming someone else for the pain you feel. "The accident was his fault." That explains your stressful situation and lifts the burden of responsibility from you. But it also makes you angry with the person you're blaming.

Furthermore you feel powerless to change the real world to your ideal world. So again you attempt to understand your helpless feeling by blaming someone else for the non-fit between real and ideal. "It's her fault that this marriage is falling apart." Blaming the other also takes you off the hook from having to change or work harder to make the real situation match your idealized one.

Finally, blaming thoughts flow naturally from demanding thoughts. When you can't change a situation by demanding it be different, then you begin to blame someone else for causing the problem. You can even assign motives to that person's misbehavior, as well as crediting characteristics to his personality. Then not only is it "his fault," but "He did it on purpose to hurt me, because he is such a revengeful person." Now, that kind of thinking will make you angry.

Now you know the ingredients of anger and how it gets started.

In Chapter Two you will discover the positive and negative ways anger is used. It serves a variety of purposes, some that work for you and others that work against you.

Chapter Two

The Uses of Anger

L ike all of your emotions, anger has a number of purposes, some positive and others negative. It may not work well in a given situation, but you can always understand why it's there. Let's take a look at the many reasons anger rises up in you.

You use anger to get the real world to match your ideal world.

This is what we've been talking about. Anger serves as a lever you place under the real, messy world in order to shove it up to meet your ideal world. Your ideal world says your children should come home at the appointed time. They do not. Your anger attempts to pry them from their "disobedient" position and get them to behave as you insist.

Anger reinforces your hold on the ideal world by denying the real world.

Anger is a pushing-away emotion. If you don't like Ann's assertive behavior, for example, your anger shoves her away from you. It also denies her assertiveness by invalidating it. You say, "Look how she behaved in that meeting. It was just terrible. No one should be that forward and demanding. She's never going to get anywhere in this company if she keeps that up." The more you insist on how Ann should have behaved, the more you deny how she *did*, in fact, behave.

Anger serves as a way to put pressure on another person to change his or her behavior.

Marge admitted she is still angry with Bill from 12 years ago. She had to go through some minor surgery in the hospital. He claims he had a couple of important meetings that day and couldn't be there with her. She had driven herself to the hospital alone, gone through the surgery alone, recuperated alone and drove home late that same day alone! Twelve years later, whenever they argue, that topic still comes up. She says, "And furthermore, you weren't there when I needed you 12 years ago." Her anger is still strong after all these years. Why?

Simple. Because she *still* feels alone today. She holds onto the hurt and anger from 12 years ago because in her mind the same thing is happening today. She still feels he is not involved or interested in her life *today*. If Bill responded to her today by being with her, sharing with her, becoming a partner with her, making her feel like she is the top priority in his life, then she would let go of the anger from the past and the present regarding his absence in her life. With her anger Marge keeps the pressure on Bill to be more present in her life today.

Anger acts like a picket fence, protecting you against outside threats.

When someone invades your territory you fight to protect yourself, your loved ones and your belongings. Adrenaline flows at

the moment of the invasion. New strength floods your body. The
fight is on to throw out the enemy.

You set up a fence around yourself and your domain. That fence
is made up of all the rules and regulations you have for how others
should treat you. When someone breaks your rule and enters your
domain to take something from you, anger rises to the occasion. It
attempts to push the villain out and mend the fence that protects you.

Anger proves to you and to others that you exist.

Kids often misbehave to get attention. When you or I misbehave,
it's usually for the same reason. We want someone to notice. You call
your kids to supper. They don't come. You call again. No answer.
You start getting upset and begin yelling for them to come. Still no
response. Pretty soon you are screaming, stamping into the family
room and standing in front of the television, an immense figure of
power, hovering over the children, demanding they get into that
kitchen immediately. Now they know you exist.

They noticed. Your anger is the hot air you use to inflate a
seriously deflated balloon. It pumps you up. Your children cannot fail
to notice you now. Your anger has made you gigantic.

Your anger also proves to *you* that you exist. With the adrenaline
flowing, you *feel* alive – blood coursing through your body, heart
beating, muscles taut, voice booming. Yes, you do exist, darn it. You
can hear and feel yourself. You really are there after all.

Anger is a natural response to hurt and
helps protect you from pain.

If you feel hurt, I know you will feel anger too. They go together.
If there is hurt, there will be anger. It doesn't necessarily follow in
reverse. In other words, you can have anger without hurt. You may
get angry when the traffic light turns red. But you don't feel hurt.

As long as you pay attention to what you have lost from your domain, you will feel hurt. Usually the loss in these cases is to your self-esteem or the esteem others have of you. When you focus on *who* made you lose your esteem, you will get angry. That's why in broken relationships you feel hurt and anger together. When you think about losing your loved one, you feel hurt. When you think about how badly he treated you, you become angry. Anger always follows hurt.

Anger serves as an emphatic form of communication.

If you really want to make a point, yelling, screaming and waving your arms helps. Parents, coaches and preachers around the world know that. Anger makes you very present to the other person, puts you right in her face. She has to listen to you now. Baseball managers, disagreeing with an umpire's call, get three inches from the ump's face and scream. They dramatically demonstrate the communication function of anger.

Anger is a powerful way of telling someone something. When people express their anger to you, it helps to heed their emotional state rather than their words. Their emotional state tells you they have something important to say to you and want you to listen well. If you don't listen well, they will stay angry and try to tell you again and again. Anger means to "over-stand" someone. The best was to handle over-standing is through understanding.

Seeing anger in others means you need to become a good listener. When you are angry, it means you want to be a talker, telling someone something important to you.

Anger, then, serves important purposes. It is primarily a protective emotion, one that keeps you safe by pushing threats away. While it looks like an attacking response, it is more often, in fact, a defensive tactic. Unfortunately, while anger protects you, it often has very negative effects on you and on your relationships. Because of these negative effects, you need to learn ways of reducing your anger and using it only in constructive and productive ways. Let's look now at the principles and tools for reducing anger.

Chapter Three

Principles and Tools for Reducing Anger

Principle 1

Do not label anger as good or bad, right or wrong. Rather, see it as helpful or not helpful.

Teachers, preachers and parents have regularly taught that some emotions are good, others are bad. Most likely you have learned that calmness is good, anxiety is unfortunate and anger is bad. Well, I want you to unlearn that teaching.

Feelings have no morality. They are neither right nor wrong, good nor bad. Anger is not terrible, nor is it particularly wonderful. At certain times it may help you, at other times it clearly hurts you. The more important question about anger is: Does it assist you in some way, or does it sabotage you? The second question is: Does it help or hurt others?

The "moral" issue around anger arises more from the *expression* of anger than from the fact of it. Just feeling angry does not seem to bother most of us. But its expression does. The "right-wrong" adjectives are directed at the way we let that anger out.

By applying moral adjectives to the feeling of anger, you place a burden of blame on yourself. It's not a difficult step to go from "My anger is bad" to "I am bad for having bad anger." Look instead only at anger's usefulness. It's not a moral issue to have the feeling of anger. If you act out the anger in a hurtful way to yourself or others, then you have a moral issue. For example, murdering someone out of anger is clearly wrong.

By now you know that having anger is normal, common and ordinary. As discussed above, anger serves a variety of purposes. At times you need it in your life. How long you hold onto it and what you do with it makes it helpful or not helpful. Anger works well in certain instances, such as attempting to persuade and motivate a person. Sometimes it can help you get your way. It can aid you in defending yourself against a threatening force. It can push you to higher levels of achievement.

On the other hand, anger can eat you up inside, especially if it grinds away for a long time. It can destroy relationships. It can cause other people to dig in their heels and resist your persuasive efforts. It can cause physical harm and death.

So, you help yourself by seeing your anger as useful or not. Ask whether your anger works for you or against you rather than asking whether it is right or wrong. If you decide it works against you, then you can work to reduce or eliminate it from your life.

Principle 2

Realize that *you* create your own anger, therefore *you* can control it.

Herein lies the fundamental principle of managing your anger. If you are to take charge of your anger and learn to reduce and eliminate it, then you need to realize that *you* created it in the first place. Nobody else "makes" you angry. I know we all talk as if things outside us make us angry. You say, "My kids make me so mad some times." Or "My boss drives me right up the wall." Or "My boyfriend really makes me upset when he says those things." You easily place the cause of your anger outside of you. When you do that, you lose control over your anger.

If you believe your anger is caused by other people or situations, then you are powerless to do anything about it except perhaps eliminate those people or situations. Of course, this isn't always possible. You give up power when you place the cause of your anger outside of yourself. No, you cause your own anger. And because you do, you can also take charge of your anger and learn to control it.

Think about it. If your anger is really caused by outside forces, then those forces should have the power to cause anger in everyone who meets up with them. If you're angry because Joan came late for the meeting, then everyone at the meeting should be equally as angry. But that is not the case. Some people don't seem upset at all. In fact, some might enjoy the fact that Joan is late, because it gives them a little time to visit with each other or better prepare the reports they are to give at the meeting.

So the cause of your anger is not outside of you. It's smack dab inside, in your thinking, in the way you view a situation and react to it. Certainly it takes a stressful situation to get your thinking going. But your anger is triggered by your own thinking about that stressful circumstance.

This realization will help you retake power over your anger. You are in charge of your anger. You created it, so you can change it. You will do so by first understanding your thoughts about stressful situations, deciding which ones make sense and which don't, and then challenging and changing those that don't make sense. Realizing you create your own anger generates the power you need to master this strong emotion.

Principle 3

**Identify, challenge and change those beliefs
that create your anger.**

Years ago Albert Ellis, Ph.D., one of the pioneers of cognitive psychology, laid out a little schema that helps you understand how you create and reduce your anger. He described it as the ABCs of rational thinking. Here are his steps in the process:

A. Activating event: Clerk in store treats you rudely.

B. Beliefs, thoughts: You think, "This person should not treat me this way. He shouldn't be allowed to work here. This is just terrible. I'll never shop in this stupid store again." These thoughts lead to . . .

C. Consequences – emotional and behavioral: Anger rises up in you. It feels as though it's caused by the dumb clerk, but in fact it comes from your beliefs about the dumb clerk.

D. Dispute: To reduce your anger, you need to challenge the beliefs you have about the clerk. You say to yourself, "I *wish* this person had not treated me this way. Perhaps he had a hard day, perhaps some personal difficulty is going on for him. I'd like to try giving him the benefit of the doubt. If I knew everything about him, I would probably understand why he acted rudely and accept him that way. Furthermore, in the great scheme of life's events, how important is this encounter anyway?"

E. Effect: The result of disputing your triggering beliefs is a gradual reduction in your anger and an increased state of calm.

The reduction of anger and increased calm, however, doesn't happen easily. It takes work and perseverance. The thoughts that come to you in Step B above seem automatic. They race right in, frequently without you even knowing it. They simply sit in you. At the right moment they pop up and create your angry feeling.

So it takes some work to get in touch with your thoughts. When you get angry, you need to pay close attention to what you are thinking. Ask yourself while you are angry or immediately afterward: What thoughts are passing through me that would be leading to this anger? Then, once you identify them, begin challenging them, attempting to replace them with more realistic and accepting thoughts. But keep in mind that just because you are trying to think differently, the anger does not automatically go away. Those old thoughts have been around for a long time and do not simply roll over and play dead as soon as new thoughts appear on the scene.

The old thoughts keep triggering the angry feelings. You put in new thoughts to challenge the old, but the angry feelings remain. You think: "Gee, this was a neat theory, but it doesn't work. I still feel angry." Then you're tempted to throw out the new thoughts and go right back to the old beliefs. Don't do that. Stick with the new thoughts challenging the old. The new thoughts have to gradually break down the old thoughts *before* the angry feelings begin to fall away. Only when the old thoughts are knocked out does the anger dissipate. Then the new thoughts beget the new feeling of calm. You need patience and a willingness to keep up the fight against your old, anger-producing thoughts.

Principle 4

Challenge the shoulds, oughts, musts and have to's.

Karen Horney, a renowned psychiatrist, called demanding thinking "the tyranny of the shoulds." These dirty words of psychology – should, ought, must and have to – cause more problems than a flock of geese heading toward an airplane engine. They generate anger faster than any other set of thoughts. They demand and insist that life be conducted in certain defined ways.

As I have shown throughout this book, your insistence that reality measure up to your ideal is the source of your anger. To break the hold anger has in your life, you need to recognize all the *demands* you make and then begin the process of changing them to *wishes*. You can no longer insist that the world and all the people in it must meet your expectations of how things should happen. You need to let go of your demands and learn to wish for your ideal, even work for it. When you cannot get the reality to match your ideal, you then need to *accept* the way things are.

First, listen to your external and internal language. Identify the "shoulds, oughts, musts and have to's." Write them down if that helps. You will be amazed at how frequently you use these words. Sense the feel of such words – the demand, the urgency, the insistence. Then stop yourself and try hard to realize that you can only demand in those circumstances where you have the power to enforce your rules. If you have no power, then challenge your demands. Throw them out. Change them to graceful wishes.

In particular, be willing to throw out the rules you make *after the fact*. The deed is done, and then you make up a rule. Your neighbor's water drain pipe runs over onto your lawn. You get angry after it happens, and you make up a rule: "My neighbor's drain pipe should not run excess water onto my lawn." Before it happened, you never even thought about it. After the fact, you make the law. Wait! There is no "should" about it. There is simply a fact: his water pipe is draining onto your lawn. You may wish it were not happening that way, but reality hits you square in the face – it is the way it is. At this moment it helps to say to yourself, "Life is the way it is, not the way I insist it must be."

If you don't like it that way, you can certainly attempt to change it. You can go talk with your neighbor about the problem. You can move the pipe yourself. You can dig a little trench to route the water back onto his property. But you can do all of those things without anger by not making a law about the pipe after the fact. Simply accept the reality as it is and then try to change it calmly.

Just as "right and wrong" are dirty words in psychology, so are "should, ought, must and have to." Try to eliminate them from your active vocabulary. Over the years I have taught people to get rid of those words. Because I have stressed it so much, I have learned myself not to think in those terms and not use those words. Now, every time I hear a "should" pop up in my inner speech, I flinch. It actually feels as though I'm swearing in public. Whenever I hear someone else say they "ought" to do something, I feel a moment's discomfort, like I would feel if someone began cursing in front of my mother. I'm probably too sensitive to those words now, but I find I don't get angry as much anymore, either.

Principle 5

Challenge the *shoulds* by believing:
" In the great scheme of life's events, this event is not that important."

Thirteen-year-old Tony left the power lawn mower running while he went into the house for a glass of water. When he came out, his eyes fixed on a two-car, one-lawn-mower traffic accident. Apparently he left the mower in drive, and it took a little spin out onto the road. An oncoming car spotted the lawn mower at the last second, swerved left to avoid hitting it and banged into a car coming from the other direction. The lawn mower continued on, banging into both cars as they came to a serious stop.

Naturally, the drivers were angry at Tony. Dad and Mom came running outside to see what happened. When informed, they, too, became angry with Tony. Fortunately, no one was injured. Insurance covered the damages. Two weeks later Dad and Mom were at a social event, retelling the story of Tony's runaway lawn mower. Everyone at the party, including Tony's parents, got a kick out of the incident. Tony's misfortune became the hit of the party. A year later that story became entrenched in the family tradition. Every time it was told the relatives laughed harder than the time before. You see, in the great scheme of life's events, that accident was not a big deal.

Certainly the incident seemed a big deal at the time. But viewed with a wide-angle lens, it took on lesser proportions and fit more gracefully against the landscape of time.

Anger is diminished the more you see the big picture. Someone whose father just died told me recently: "A terrible event like death makes you realize how insignificant so many other things are. It seems a small thing now to get upset over so much dinky stuff in life." This woman had a broader perspective.

If you get angry easily, it's partly because you use your telescopic lens to see. You zero in on the offense. You block out all the background. A telescopic lens make the object look much bigger than it actually is. That's what your dramatic thinking does in creating anger. To reduce your anger, use your wide-angle lens. Then you see the object of your anger with all the landscape behind it. In that frame the issue looks smaller, less significant. You "de-dramatize" your thinking and free yourself from demanding that it "should be different."

So when you hear those dramas and demands racing through your head, when the situation in front of you feels gigantic and awful, try challenging your thinking with: "In the great scheme of life's events, this event is not that important."

Principle 6

**The more you *accept* reality,
the less angry you become.**

I know. You want reality to fit your dream world. The weather should be sunny and in the middle 70s. The bugs should be dormant.

No dogs should bark. Your neighbors should always be kind and friendly. Your loved one should always be sensitive to your needs. And you should win the lottery.

Then there's reality.

You reduce your anger the more you focus on your reality and the less you keep insisting that your ideals be met. You give power to what you focus on. By focusing on your ideal, you will continually demand that reality fit your perfect image of life. Your daily living becomes a fight to force reality to change. Instead, you can learn to focus on your reality and accept it as it is – some of it satisfying, some of it not so satisfying and some of it neutral.

Some people object to this notion. They claim having ideals is good. I agree. I have no problem with goals and dreams, plans for achievement and wonderful visions of the future. As long as you have the executive power to make those visions come true, good for you. Work for them. Strive. Achieve. But if you don't have executive power, if your ideal images cannot be achieved, then don't keep insisting they "must be" realized. Then accept your reality.

As I tell people all the time, "You can make as many laws, rules and regulations as you want. But there is one law you cannot make and insist on being followed. It is the law that says 'Every law I make ought to be obeyed.'" So you can have dreams, but you cannot insist on everyone and everything else following those dreams. Ashley Brilliant, an author and syndicated cartoonist, once said, "Just because I accept you as you are, does not mean I have abandoned all hope of your improving." You, too, need to accept the limitations of reality. But you can continue to *hope* that reality changes. You simply cannot *demand* that it change.

An interesting thing occurs when you reach stages of acceptance in your life. Your anger dissipates. You cannot be accepting and angry at the same time. If you accept the limitedness of your computer consultant when he installs your word processing system, you won't get angry with him when the "Caps Lock" function doesn't work right. You won't get as angry with your husband when you learn to accept his expressions of love in the form of fixing the car and working hard on the job. You won't get as upset with your wife when you accept that her compulsive house cleaning comes from a person-ality glitch that is more an illness than a willful act to annoy you.

Acceptance and understanding are the perfect antidotes to anger. You come to acceptance by 1) focusing on reality, 2) recognizing that everything and everyone has strengths and weaknesses, and 3) saying yes to both the strengths and weaknesses. The best way to come to such acceptance is by starting with yourself. I know this may be hard to handle, but even you have a bright side and a dark side. The more you face both aspects of yourself and learn to appreciate yourself as you are – a limited, but wonderful human being – the less angry you will be toward others. If you learn self-acceptance, then you will find yourself much more accepting and tolerant of others' reality. That acceptance leads to high degrees of flexibility, which keeps you from anger and leads you to peace of mind.

Principle 7

To challenge angry beliefs about another, lay out that person's history and walk through it.

Understanding leads to acceptance. Acceptance reduces anger. So to decrease your anger try to gain more understanding of the "enemy." But how can you do that, since you don't always have access to more information? If a store clerk – a perfect stranger to you – treats you badly, it's pretty hard to sit down with her and ask for her history so you can better understand her behavior. You probably don't want to understand her anyway. You'd just as soon be angry with her for 10 minutes as you drive home, let the anger die and get on with life. Fine.

But in other instances, your anger doesn't drift away so easily. It centers on people who are more significant to you than the store clerk. With these people it's worth it to you to reduce your anger by further understanding.

Start by believing that everyone has a history and that history influences his or her behavior today. There are always perfectly good reasons for people to act the way they do. You simply don't know all those reasons. If you did, you would not be angry with them for what they are doing. Most anger, in fact, arises from *misunderstanding*.

A new supervisor comes on the work scene. He has a different style than Joe had. This man, Mike, claims he wants open communication, but his way of doing that is by sending memos. Joe had roamed the plant, talking with everyone. Mike's memos seem so impersonal. It feels like communication is cut off. You no longer feel you have access to the boss. Some of the memos call for changes in procedure. You begin to feel powerless. You gradually become angry with this cold, aloof supervisor. Eventually you can't stand him. You can't understand why he communicates the way he does. So you come to a conclusion about him. "He's basically an insecure person. He shouldn't be a supervisor. He's destroying everything we have built here."

To reduce those demanding and dramatic thoughts, you have to understand that Mike has a history. If you could get inside his life and walk through it from infancy on, his manner of communicating today would make perfect sense to you. If you knew how his father and mother communicated, what he observed as a child, what he experienced as a teenager; if you could understand his mental processes, his feeling reactions to other people; if you could know his experiences of rejection and friendship; if you could be aware of all the dynamics that led him to this day and this behavior, you would say about it, "That makes sense. I understand why Mike communicates this way."

You might still not *like* it. That's fine. You don't have to like his behavior. But you do need to understand that there is a perfectly sensible history to explain that behavior.

By understanding Mike's history, you let go of your anger. As soon as you say, "I understand why he acts that way," you will not say, "He *shouldn't* act that way." If you understand, you will not demand his behavior to be different. You may *wish* it were different ("I liked working for Joe better than I do Mike"), but with understanding you will accept Mike's behavior more graciously.

Many times you do not have the opportunity to actually lay out someone's history and walk through it with that person. But you can still know that such a history is there. When you become angry with that person, try to realize that she has a history, and if you knew it, her behavior would be perfectly understandable. To help you understand, you can even guess at what that history might be. You might speculate on her situation that leads her to be so crabby most mornings: "Ann must have a hard time getting all her children ready for school before coming to work." Or "Maybe she's used to everything being in place when she gets to work." Or "Perhaps when she was a child, her mom responded to stress by getting crabby."

Such speculations can be helpful if you don't lock in on them as fact but simply use them to help you respond to her in a more understanding and sympathetic way. The point is, everyone has a history, a perspective and a set of beliefs coming out of that history that influence and shape the way that person responds today. If you have all that information about people, you would reduce your anger greatly. Even if you don't have that information, you know it's there. Give people the benefit of the doubt. Tell yourself, "If I understood all that lies behind this behavior, it would make sense." If something makes sense, you won't be insisting that it be different.

Principle 8

Challenge blaming thoughts by realizing that people act badly out of stupidity, ignorance or disturbance and rarely out of malice.

"It's his fault." "She is so self-centered." "He is totally insensitive." "She is actually evil the way she responds." When you hear these and other blaming thoughts, a bell should go off in your head. Warning: These blaming thoughts are making you angry. Furthermore, they are not accurate anyway. Try changing your blaming thoughts to more accepting thoughts.

It is very easy, for instance, to blame a rapist, an alcoholic, a bank robber, an arrogant boss or a hostile cop for their behavior. It's a snap to label them mean or vicious. That, of course, gives you license to remain angry with them. While these people need to be held *responsible* for their actions, they, in fact, are not mean or vicious at all. They have very low IQs or don't know what's going on or are psychologically disturbed.

The father who sexually abuses his daughter is both ignorant and psychologically disturbed. He is not an evil person. The alcoholic is not a bad man but an ill person who desperately needs help. When you view people and their behavior in this way, you free yourself from blaming, which in turn reduces anger.

Wives often blame their husbands for their unhappy marriages. They claim their husbands are insensitive, self-centered and immature. They don't like these men anymore. And, they claim, it's the husband's fault that the couple has not achieved deep intimacy in marriage. On the contrary. these husbands are limited in their ability to achieve intimacy. They may have very low IQ's. But generally that's not the case. They may be psychologically disturbed, but that, too, is usually not so. They are ignorant when it comes to intimacy. They simply don't know how to do it the way their wives do it. I don't demand that a six-year-old child rattle off algebraic formulas. I don't insist that a 50-year-old American speak Russian without training. Those are limitations in the six and 50-year-old. These people are not bad because of their limitations. They are just ignorant and limited. In the same way, if these wives continue insisting that their spouses are bad men because of their limitations around intimacy, they are in for long years of frustration, anger and resentment.

Principle 9

Challenge the *fairness* belief by realizing you simply have needs that are not being met.

Remember, "fair" and "unfair" get you angry. "Unfair" means the world has not given you what you wanted. It has not lived up to your expectation of how things should be. When you label something as "unfair," you add fuel to your angry fire. Not only are you not getting what you wanted, but you are complaining that you "should" have gotten it and that the entire system is unjust and bad for not giving it to you.

In the future when you hear yourself claiming "unfair," try using that word as a *signal* indicating you need something and are not getting it. Pay attention more to what you need than to how unjust the world is toward you. As parents and teachers have proclaimed throughout the ages, "Nobody ever said the world would be fair." What they meant was, "Nobody ever said you would get all your needs met." Somehow it seems easier to accept the second statement than the first. You can appreciate that all your needs will not be met. But you really have to swallow hard to acknowledge that the world does not always act in a fair way. You believe you're fair. So, of course, the rest of the world should act fairly, too, right? Wrong.

It's also helpful to realize that other people always think they are acting fairly. You have an argument with a store clerk about the price of a jar of applesauce. The jar was mistakenly labeled 40 cents less than it should have been. You buy the jar at the price marked, but the checker rings it up at the proper price. What's fair? Who's cheating? Just as you think you are acting fairly by demanding the 40 cents off because the label said so, the clerk thinks she is acting fairly by informing you of the stock boy's mistake. In her mind it's unfair for the company to lose money just because the stock boy erred in marking the jar.

You believe the store is acting unfairly. But you need to realize that the clerk sincerely believes she is responding fairly and further believes that *you* are acting unfairly. By realizing that both of you think you are acting fairly, you can often take the discussion out of the realm of "fair" and "unfair" and move it to the area of what you both *need* from this situation.

Principle 10

**Do not dramatize your frustrations.
Instead, stay close to reality.**

In college I roomed with Bernie who loved living in crisis. Everything was wonderful or awful, bizarre, incredible, needed to be discussed immediately, couldn't wait until the morning, or was lost for all time. I got caught up in his crises feeling the strain and tension right along with him. After living in a state of high anxiety for a semester, I couldn't take it any longer. I talked with a wise professor who gave me simple, good advice. He said I should pour a gallon of water on whatever Bernie said and add a pound of salt. Then I was probably getting close to the reality. Once I began applying that formula I mellowed out and got along better with Bernie.

If you find anger flooding your body and your mind more than you'd like, look to your dramatic thoughts. If you hear the nevers and alwayses, the awfuls and incredibles, then you might want to use the formula I used to deal with Bernie. Pour the cold water of reality onto your traumatic view and dump a good dose of salt on your "awesome" conclusions about what's going on.

It's hard to hear your own dramatic and catastrophic thinking because you naturally believe your thoughts are in perfect harmony with reality. However, if you find yourself getting upset and angry regularly, then don't trust that your thoughts are in touch with the real world. You can bet you're spinning off dramatic and powerful thoughts that are fueling your anger.

To challenge your dramatic thinking, ask yourself "If I had a video camera, what would that camera be picking up right now?" See as a video camera sees. The camera is objective and realistic. That's what you want. Throw out anything the camera can't see. Then you will shave your powerful thoughts down to size. By reducing your drama, you also reduce your anger.

Principle 11

Make sure you take responsibility for getting your own needs met as best as you can.

Your anger signals an expectation or a need that is not being met. You want a closer relationship with your friend but don't have it. You feel like you're doing all the work to make it happen. She never initiates. You get hurt and then angry. Use that anger as a sign, telling you what you need – closeness. Focus on your desire for a more intimate relationship rather than focusing on her for not granting it.

Then *you* work to make it happen. In that way you use your anger as a motivating energy, converting it into action to help you get what you want.

By focusing on your friend and her lack of sensitivity, you keep your anger alive. Furthermore, you stop yourself from taking action. If you think she took intimacy away from you or it's *her* fault for your being sad, then you render yourself helpless. In that frustrated state, your anger grows like algae in a stagnant pond.

When anger rises up in you, *you* need to take responsibility for the anger and for meeting the need you have under the anger. Don't focus on how the other is failing to fill your need. Concentrate instead on taking action to make sure your needs are met.

Principle 12

**To keep your cool, validate your position
as well as the other person's position.**

Given your Western heritage, you most likely think logically and precisely. You put similar items in the same category and opposing elements in opposite categories. In your mind black cannot be white and wrong cannot be right. In an argument if one position is correct, then the other must be incorrect. Correct?

Not necessarily! What if you are both correct? In fact, from each of your points of view, you are both expressing what you experience as the truth. Your view certainly reflects what you believe to be an accurate statement of reality, but so does the other person's view of his reality. The most helpful belief in reducing anger in this kind of situation is: *Both views are valid, they are only different.*

When you argue with another person, your effort is to persuade that person of the rightness of your position. When he isn't persuaded, you use anger to enforce your view. In the process you attempt to invalidate his view. It can't be his way because it's your way. And that's that. Actually, you are both trying to persuade each other of the correctness of your views. Anger forces the issue. One of you must be right, the other wrong.

In fact, both views are legitimate, valid and understandable. By realizing that your position is valid and can stand as okay, you don't need to defend it against the persuasive onslaught of the other. You need only to recognize that he believes his point of view as firmly as you believe yours. And when you look at it from his angle, you can appreciate how he can come to that conclusion.

Unfortunately, you and I grew up learning the opposite belief. We learned that in an argument one person is right and the other wrong. Our legal system reinforces that belief by setting up a judge to determine who wins and who loses. We live our life in either-ors.

Brian came downstairs from his bedroom at 9:00 p.m. after going to bed an hour earlier. As he came down he called out, "Daddy, Mommy . . . " Dad, sitting in the living room reading the paper, snapped, "What are you doing up young man? You climb right back up those stairs and get to bed."

Brian tried again, "Yeah, but Dad . . . "

"No buts about it, young man. You get in that bed and sleep. You have school tomorrow," answered Dad.

So Brian trudged back upstairs and plopped into bed. What he learned from that little encounter was simple but powerful: "When my opinion differs from Dad's, only his counts. My view doesn't matter. It's not valid."

But clearly that's not true. Brian's view was just as valid as Dad's. Dad simply expressed his view in a stronger way. Brian was sick and threw up in bed. That was his reality. Very valid, indeed. So was Dad's view. He wanted Brian sleeping so he could better function at school tomorrow. Two differing views, both valid. They could have stood together.

So Brian grows up still believing, as many of us have done, that when two people differ, only one position counts. Not true. Challenge that belief in yourself. Hold onto your own view as valid, but also accept that the other person's position is valid for him as well. That allows you to slow down and make the effort to understand the other person rather than try *winning* this contest of who's right and who's wrong.

Principle 13

**Try to attach your anger to immediate stressors
rather than to the personality of the other.**

Connect your anger to what you're not getting or to what doesn't fit. Stay away from applying it to any characteristics of the other person. If you choose to be angry, aim your anger at feeling misunderstood rather than at the jerk who can't understand. Direct it toward the inconvenience you experience by having to return a garment to a store rather than the total incompetence of the store owner. Be upset with the spilt milk, but try not to focus on how absolutely clumsy your child is.

When you focus on qualities in the other person, you become helpless, which only aggravates frustration. You can't do anything about someone who is incompetent, selfish, insensitive, stupid or emotionally impoverished. But you can do something when you focus on your own needs, on what is not fitting out there, and what you can do to change the situation. You empower yourself by paying attention to what you need and are not getting rather than on how awful the other person is.

You reduce your anger when you focus on what you lost or need, not on the one causing you the loss or failing to fill your need. By doing so, you may feel more sadness, but you will reduce your anger.

Principle 14

Forgiving and apologizing wipe away anger.

It's hard to admit you are wrong. But when you do, your anger vanishes in an instant. Recently I got angry with my daughter for leaving her cereal bowl on the counter, only to find out later my wife was the culprit. I had no anger toward my wife because I figured she just didn't get around to it. But I was angry at my daughter when I thought she had done it because she does it all the time. When I found out Amy didn't do it, I apologized to her and realized my anger had disappeared.

As you can see from this example, apology and forgiveness come from understanding. The more information you have, the more you appreciate the other person's position and will apologize or forgive. When someone "wrongs" you, anger rises up as a protector against his invasion. But when you come to further understand why he did what he did, you let go of your rigid position and eliminate your anger.

I wish people felt freer to apologize and forgive. Often I hear couples relate past hurts to one another. I try to get one to understand the other. When she does understand him, I expect her to say quickly, "Gee, George, I am really sorry for that. I never realized it meant so much to you for me to be at your business conferences with you." But that rarely happens. Instead, she defends why she didn't go or blames him for not asking directly enough. If he still feels hurt and angry because she didn't go with him 10 years ago, a sincere apology does more to release his anger than any effort to justify her position.

Saying you're sorry doesn't mean you lose, he wins. It simply means you recognize his hurt, you realize his upset and you feel badly that he feels badly. Keep your ego out of it. You're not in competition

with your friend. You're in a relationship that needs to be strength-
ened at the moment.

Forgiveness and sorrow tell the other that anger is being set aside,
and reconciliation is the order of the day. To forgive means to
reconnect. To express sorrow means that you understand the other's
hurt, which helps that person let go of his hurt and the anger that goes
with it.

By following the principles presented in this chapter, you will go
a long way in reducing and controlling your anger. Now let's talk
about ways of expressing anger so this powerful emotion works for
you instead of against you.

Chapter Four

Principles and Tools for Expressing Anger

F eeling angry is one thing, *expressing* it is quite another. In this book I have talked mostly about ways of reducing your anger. But once the anger is there, what can you do with it? Should you hold it in and simply try to contain it? Should you unload your anger on others? Should you keep smiling even if you're furious? Here are a few principles that help you answer these questions:

Principle 1

Express your anger directly when you think it will work for you and the other.

Some parental anger works well in urging kids along. Teachers and coaches get angry at times, and it motivates children to work harder. Bosses become angry to get more productivity. Customers use anger to get better service.

If you express anger, don't make it a personal attack. When anger moves to the personal level, it almost always has a negative effect on the relationship. It invades the other person's space and cannot easily be taken back. You can tell an employee in no uncertain terms about an inadequate report. Such an intense expression may well motivate the person to do better. But if you say he is "an incompetent oaf," you have crossed a line from which there is no return. Now you have made a statement about him, not just his work. That kind of anger is never helpful.

Also, the direct expression of anger works if it's not too frequent. If you're forever on your daughter's case in an angry way, she *will* start backing away from you. So if you decide to express your anger, do it infrequently. It has a much more positive effect (people will be surprised and will listen up), and it won't drive them away from you.

Principle 2

Express your anger in a way the other can receive it.

The expression of strong anger is usually seen as an attack. If you explode at someone, he instinctively backs away. The anger gets in the way of the message you are sending. He focuses on the anger, not the message.

When I was involved in Little League baseball, we had a coach whose anger was legendary. No kids wanted to play for him; no parents wanted their kids to play for him; volunteer umpires refused to officiate his games. His expression of anger did not work. No one paid attention to his message. We all focused on his anger and backed away. He didn't express his anger in a way anyone could receive it.

For another person to receive your anger, you must have your anger under control. Anger that appears out of control scares other people and causes them to back up and defend. In that position they cannot listen well. So you need to modify your anger. Make sure your initial surge of adrenaline has passed before you talk. Put a little space between your first burst of anger and your expression of it.

Second, talk about the problem *you* are having at the moment. Make your expression a revelation of self and not an attack on the faults of the other. Start by saying, "I'm really having a problem with the way our relationship is going. I feel alone more than I want to. And I look to you for that special companionship. Sometimes I feel hurt about that, and other times I get angry about it. I really want a close feeling with you."

In this case you have talked about yourself. You have gotten your message across in a way the other can receive it, and you have told her you were angry. But you put it in the context of the whole message and made it easier for her to hear.

Principle 3

Don't express your anger directly if it pushes the other person away (unless that's what you want).

Anger is a shoving-away emotion. It protects you but tends to alienate the other. When you get angry, try to pause. In the pause, decide whether your anger will hurt your relationship or help it. If you decide it will hurt, then don't express the anger directly. Go in search of the need not being met under the anger and try to express that need. But the anger must be checked because it will push the other away.

This is particularly true in family relationships. Too much anger directed toward children keeps them from you. Eventually they learn not to talk to Dad and Mom because "They will just get upset anyway." The same thing happens in marriage. The wife complains that her husband never talks to her. But the husband says every time he opens his mouth, she blows him out of the water. He has learned to back up and stay away.

You need to express your feelings, but don't get caught in the old pop psychology approach that called for "brutal honesty." While honesty is important in a relationship, it must be tempered with respect and a sensitivity for preserving and enriching the relationship. It is definitely not helpful to "put it out there the way I feel it." No. You first need to decide whether your angry expression will help or hurt your relationship. Then proceed with caution and regard for the other.

Principle 4

When you get angry, acknowledge it and accept it.
Don't repress it. Then decide what to do with it.

The argument from the "brutally honest" school runs like this: "If you don't express your anger, it will get buried deep within you and start to eat away at your insides. It's not healthy to repress your anger. That's how you get ulcers."

Certainly repressing feelings does not work well. Denying your anger, pushing it down over long periods of time does cause psychological and oftentimes physical difficulties. Your husband comes into the kitchen with a deep frown cut into his face, grumbling under his breath. He gets a glass out of the cabinet and slams the door, rattling the dishes inside. You innocently ask, "Are you angry about something?" To which he replies, "No, I'm not angry and don't bother me."

Worse yet is the person who always smiles, shows that wonderful calm exterior and says "yes" to every request everyone makes of her. Yet underneath, she is unhappy and resenting the demands put on her. Dealing with anger in these ways is not helpful.

Admit to yourself that you're angry. Notice it, attend to it. Let yourself seethe a little. Then decide what you want to do with it. You may conclude not to express your anger to the one offending you because it won't work. That's fine. You're not *repressing* your anger. You paid attention to it. You know it's there. You own it. You are, however, deciding to *suppress* the expression of the anger directly to the person. You, then, are in charge of your anger and its expression.

Principle 5

Once you own your anger, you control its expression.

When you feel angry, you often experience a strong physical urge to do something expressive. You want to yell, kick, punch, stab or shoot. To simply acknowledge your anger and let it stay inside doesn't seem enough. The urge to release the anger remains strong. It feels temporarily good to "get it out." So, how can you get it out without directly blasting the offender?

Here are some options for you:

1. Express your anger to a third party. But try not to express it to every and any third party. Pick a good friend, one who can hold confidences and share your upset. If you find yourself running around to everyone at work, unloading your anger about the boss, you are hurting your relationships with the boss and the other workers. You are also reinforcing your anger rather than getting rid of it. The more you talk about it, the more power you give it. Talking about your anger does not reduce it. It satisfies, temporarily, your urge to strike out. But expressing the anger tends to keep you focused on the stressor and the thoughts that created the anger.

2. Write out your anger. Many psychologists recommend that you put your thoughts and feelings about a particular stressor on paper. You're angry with your father over his

treatment of you when you were a child. To express your
anger directly and verbally to your father now might only
make matters worse. So, instead, you write a letter to your
father – one that is never sent – telling him all you feel and
believe.

3. Shout out your anger to the world. Some people find it
    helpful to go to a lake shore or a forest or a wide-open field
    and yell and scream as loud as they can. This approach
    serves a positive purpose, especially when people have
    not been in touch with their anger and have tried to hold
    it back all their lives. I suggest, at times, that people use
    their cars to yell. The car is a great therapy office. Two
    cautions, however: If you express anger in the car, do it
    when you are alone; second, be careful about driving and
    screaming. Don't take out your anger on other cars!

4. Strenuous physical activity can help burn off the adrena-
    line. People report that jogging helps them release anger.
    Walking, chopping wood, aerobics, tennis, racquet ball
    are all activities that allow the physical pressure of anger
    to be vented. Those activities also shift your focus to a
    piece of wood or a ball or a dog chasing you while you jog.

In all of these activities realize that you are *temporarily* releasing
some angry feelings. That release can feel momentarily good. It's
like lancing an infection. It releases the pressure. However, if you
don't treat the infection directly, the pressure redevelops. The same
is true with your anger. Simply releasing the pressure doesn't reduce
your anger. To give up the anger, you have to apply the principles
talked about throughout this book. You need to alter your anger
thoughts and your point of view.

Imagine that you're angry with your mother because in your
childhood she responded to you in a cold and distant way. Her
responses have had various negative effects on how you now relate
to women. As you become more aware of her relationship to you, you

become more angry. You release your anger by beating a pillow and talking with a therapist. But the anger keeps returning. It will always remain as long as you continue to *view* your mother in the same way.

You have to change your beliefs about your mother, letting go of such thoughts as: "It wasn't fair that I ended up with such a cold mother." "She should never have had so many kids." "She should have stayed home once in a while." "She has messed up my entire life." These kinds of beliefs keep the anger alive and kicking. No matter how frequently you *express* your anger, it will return as long as your beliefs remain in place.

Venting your feelings to another or into the wind serves the purpose of getting in touch with the feelings. When you hear your own anger, it offers you a good barometer of your feeling. Now you know what that gnawing feeling is. You also hear some of your thinking behind the anger. At times you can change your thoughts about a situation just by hearing yourself talk about it. As you express your angry thoughts about a co-worker, for example, you might realize some of your views are silly, not true or overstated. As you vent to a friend, you begin seeing the situation differently, and your anger fades.

Your anger doesn't diminish because you express it. It does so because *when* you express it, you hear your triggering thoughts and you change them on the spot. Expressing your anger allows you to *see* the situation in a different way. You take away the demands, the dramas and the blames.

In summary, the three basic ways to reduce anger are:
1. Slow down your adrenaline.
2. Reduce the stressors in your life.
3. Change your angry beliefs.

Anger blends outside stressors, your beliefs about those stressors and the flow of adrenaline. You can attack your anger at any or all of these three levels.

First, you can slow down adrenaline by learning to relax and enjoy the reality of your life. Your ability to become mentally flexible, to let go of your insistence about creating the ideal world, helps you reduce the powerful flow of adrenaline – the ingredient that gives you the *feeling* of anger.

Furthermore, learning to gain *balance* in your life also helps you relax. When you become too intense in one area of life, you over-focus it and give it tremendous power. You soon begin insisting that everything in that area must go according to your plan, and you are right back into demanding thinking. Balance your work with your home life, leisure, community service, personal growth, spiritual activity and flat out fun. Nothing then becomes so important, so big, that you can't let go and get into something else. Moving away from your primary focus allows you to see it from a clearer, less dramatic perspective.

Second, reduce anger by changing the stressors in your life. If you get angry every morning because of traffic on the expressway, then drive the city streets or leave early. Or better yet, leave late. If it annoys you that the rain gutter keeps leaking, then fix it or get it fixed. If the rabbits keep eating your garden vegetables, then put a mesh fence around the garden instead of getting irritated year after year.

All anger arises because you want something out there to change. You don't like it the way it is. So in those situations where you have the executive power to change something into your ideal, do it. Let your irritation and anger motivate you to take action to make the real world meet your ideal world. But don't just sit back and say, "But I shouldn't have to be the one doing anything here." For instance, your leaky rain gutter drives you crazy. But on principle you don't fix it because it shouldn't be leaking so soon after installation. You're angry at the defective materials or the incompetent labor. You believe you shouldn't have to get up there and fix it. But if that gutter will stop leaking by you getting up there and plugging the hole, then do it so you can get on with life!

Third, and most important, you reduce and eliminate anger by recognizing that your thoughts create anger. So replacing your angry thoughts with new, more realistic thoughts offers the most effective avenue to peace of mind. When anger arises in you, look immediately to your thoughts, identify the ones that are triggering your anger and *doubt* their accuracy. Question those thoughts. Let yourself know that your way of seeing this stressful situation needs challenging. Then challenge those thoughts, trying to replace them with more calming and accurate reflections of reality. Anger happens mainly in your head. So pay attention to your *thoughts* – the source of your anger – and change those thoughts until your anger disappears.

Chapter Five

Developing this Skill with Others

Reducing your anger takes hard work. Often the journey to peace of mind is made easier by walking with other people. In this chapter I want to outline some steps you can take to manage your anger by working with another person or a group of people.

Step One

Identify your anger by telling each other about your experiences of anger. Talk about the *physical* cues that tell you anger is surfacing. What happens to your body when you get angry? Do you breathe harder? Does your heart beat faster? Do you feel warmer? The more you discuss these cues, the more you become sensitive to the internal signs that say, "Yes, I am angry now."

Step Two

Identify the stressors that lead to your anger. This is often easy to talk about. It's the part most people focus on when expressing anger. It allows you to tell what your husband did, or your children, or your friends or boss. You can narrate how the dishwasher leaked soapy water all over the kitchen or the car broke down on the expressway.

Step Three

Identify your angry thinking. Once you have reviewed some of the stressors, take one and discuss what your *idealization* of that situation was. What are the "shoulds, oughts, musts and have to's?" Help each other recognize the demanding quality of your thinking, along with the drama and the blaming. Then look at how far the reality is from the ideal – and lament a little. But not too long.

Step Four

Help each other *challenge your idealistic and demanding thinking.* This is where you really need help from one another. Of course, you believe that all your beliefs are perfectly reasonable. You need other voices to show you how unreasonable your thinking actually is. (Do not reinforce each other's demanding or dramatic thinking by agreeing with it. Fight it, challenge it, change it.)

Step Five

Try to *create a set of beliefs that reduces anger.* Make a list that includes some of the following:
   A. In the great scheme of life's events, this event is not that important.
   B. Life is as it is, not the way I insist it must be.
   C. "Should" is a dirty word.
   D. There is no law that states all reality must measure up to *my* ideals.

You might want to go through this book for more positive beliefs to add to this list in case you have trouble thinking up your own.

Step Six

Finally, you can go through this book principle by principle. Each principle and tool explained in here can serve as a topic of discussion. The more you talk about these views, the more you will come to believe them. The stronger they are in you, the more powerful they will become in helping you challenge those beliefs that cause you anger.

Conclusion

By reducing your anger, you open the door to a deeper state of calm and peace. You increase your ability to enter more intimately into the lives of those you love. If your anger is strong and dominating, the principles and tools in this book will help you take control over your anger rather than letting your anger control you.

And if your anger is mild but a bit of an annoyance, then by working with these principles you will increase your contentment and your mental flexibility. The more tolerance and acceptance you gain in life, the more enjoyment you will know. You will learn to let go of the negatives, of the mismatches between your ideal and the real. You will live more fully in the real world, with its positives and negatives. By staying in that real world of light and dark, the light will stand out the more you learn to accept the dark. By letting go of your anger, you will move naturally to live in light, peace and joy.

Appendix

Review of Principles for Reducing Anger

1. Do not label anger as good or bad, right or wrong. Rather, see it as helpful or not helpful.
2. Realize that *you* create your own anger, therefore *you* can control it.
3. Identify, challenge and change those beliefs that create your anger.
4. Challenge the shoulds, oughts, musts and have to's.
5. Challenge the "shoulds" by believing: "In the great scheme of life's events, this event is not that important."
6. The more you *accept* reality, the less angry you become.
7. To challenge angry beliefs about another, lay out that person's history and walk through it.
8. Challenge blaming thoughts by realizing that people act badly out of stupidity, ignorance or disturbance and rarely out of malice.
9. Challenge the "fairness" belief by realizing you simply have needs that are not being met.

10. Do not dramatize your frustrations. Instead, stay close to reality.
11. Make sure you take responsibility for getting your own needs met as best as you can.
12. To keep your cool, validate your position as well as the other person's position.
13. Try to attach your anger to immediate stressors rather than to the personality of the other.
14. Forgiving and apologizing wipe away anger.

Review of Principles for Expressing Anger

1. Express your anger directly when you think it will work for you and the other.
2. Express your anger in a way the other can receive it.
3. Don't express your anger directly if it pushes the other person away (unless that's what you want).
4. When you get angry, acknowledge it and accept it. Don't repress it. Then decide what to do with it.
5. Once you own your anger, you control its expression.